NATURAL WORLD

ORANGUTAN

HABITATS • LIFE CYCLES • FOOD CHAINS • THREATS

Stephen Brend

RAINTREE
STECK-VAUGHN
PUBLISHERS

A Harcourt Company

Austin   New York
www.steck-vaughn.com

NATURAL WORLD

Chimpanzee • Crocodile • Dolphin • Elephant
Giant Panda • Great White Shark • Grizzly Bear
Hippopotamus • Killer Whale • Lion • Orangutan
Penguin • Polar Bear • Tiger

Cover photo: Eye to eye with an adult male orangutan
Title page: A young orangutan
Contents page: Orangutans are excellent climbers.
Index page: Just hanging around in the treetops

Published by Raintree Steck-Vaughn Publishers, an imprint of Steck-Vaughn Company

Library of Congress Cataloging-in-Publication Data
Brend, Stephen.
Orangutan / Stephen Brend.
    p.   cm.—(Natural world)
    Includes bibliographical references and index.
    ISBN 0-7398-2765-0 (hard)
    0-7398-3126-7 (soft)
    1. Orangutan—Juvenile literature.
    [1. Orangutan.]
    I. Title. II. Series.

Printed in Italy. Bound in the United States.
1 2 3 4 5 6 7 8 9 0 04 03 02 01 00

Picture credits
Stephen Brend/IPPL 41; Bruce Coleman Collection *front cover* (John Cancalosi), 3 (Jorg and Petra Wegner), 9 (Erwin and Peggy Bauer), 11 (Christer Fredriksson), 13 (Christer Fredriksson), 15 (Gerald S. Cubitt), 17 (Christer Fredriksson), 18 (Michael P. Price), 21 (Ingo Arndt), 23, 25 (Alain Compost), 26 (Christer Fredriksson), 27, 29 (Alain Compost), 31 (Christer Fredriksson), 32, 33 (Alain Compost), 35 (John Cancalosi), 40 (Alain Compost), 44 middle (Christer Fredriksson), 45 middle, 45 bottom (Alain Compost). Digital Vision 7, 36, 37, 48; NHPA 1 (Mark Bowler), 8, 10 (B. Jones and M. Shimlock), 19 (Mark Bowler), 30 (John Shaw), 38 (Daniel Heuclin), 39 (Andy Rouse), 42, 43 (Martin Harvey), 44 top (B. Jones and M. Shimlock); The Orangutan Foundation 34 (Ian Redmond); Oxford Scientific Films 12 (Mike Hill), 14, 16 (Konrad Wothe), 24 (Michael Dick), 28 (Mike Hill), 44 bottom (Konrad Wothe); Still Pictures 22, 45 top (Cyril Rouso). Maps on page 4 by Victoria Webb and Peter Bull. All other artworks by Michael Posen.

Contents

Meet the Orangutan

Orangutans are the world's largest tree-dwelling mammals. They live in Indonesia's vast rain forests, descending to the forest floor only to eat. Their eyes, facial expressions, and the way they move their hands are so humanlike it is not surprising that their name means "person of the forest" in the Malay language.

◄ Indonesia's location on a world map

▲ The red shading on this map shows where orangutans live.

ORANGUTAN FACTS

There are two species of orangutan: the Bornean and the Sumatran. The scientific name for the Bornean orangutan is *pongo pygmaeus*. For the Sumatran, it is *pongo abelii*.

●

Adult males can reach 5 ft. (1.5 m) in height and can weigh as much as 220 lbs. (100 kg). Females are much smaller. They are about 3 ft. (1 m) tall and weigh up to 100 lbs. (45 kg).

▼ An adult male orangutan

Arms
Orangutans' arms are very strong and can be more than 3 ft. (1 m) long. This allows them to reach fruit that might be at the end of a branch too small to hold the animal's weight.

Eyes
The forward-facing eyes enable orangutans to judge distances accurately. Their eyes are dark brown, because the bright tropical sunlight would damage lighter-colored eyes.

Cheek pads
Adult males develop huge cheek pads on their face. These are often covered with scars and bite marks from fights with rival males.

Throat pouch
Males inflate the pouch to make their calls carry farther. When it is not inflated, the pouch hangs down like a double chin.

Hands
Like humans, orangutan hands have a separate thumb that sits opposite four fingers. This is called an opposable thumb. It enables them to hold and move objects. The thick fingers have fingerprints.

Coat
The orangutan's hair is usually red, but the color can vary greatly. Some orangutans may be dark brown, while others are almost blond.

Feet
Orangutans' feet are more like an extra pair of hands, because they use their feet mainly for climbing.

The Great Apes

Orangutans are a type of great ape. The great apes make up a group of mammals that all have large brains, gripping hands, and forward-facing eyes. Gorillas, chimpanzees, and bonobos are also great apes. In fact, scientists classify humans as great apes, too. Besides humans, orangutans are the only great apes found outside of Africa.

◀ The bonobo, or pygmy chimpanzee, is the smallest of the great apes. It lives in large family groups, called troops, in the rain forests of the Congo River Basin, in Central Africa.

Gorillas, chimpanzees, and bonobos sleep in trees, but they move mainly on the ground. Orangutans spend almost all their time in the trees. The African great apes live in groups, and the groups may form part of a larger community. Orangutans mostly live alone.

Orangutans live in rain forests on the Indonesian islands of Borneo and Sumatra. The rain forests are made up of tall, straight trees called diterocarps. Orangutans also live in swamp forests, which can become flooded after heavy rain. This makes the ability to move through the trees essential.

▲ Chimpanzees are humans' closest relatives in the animal kingdom. They are more closely related to humans than they are to orangutans.

An Orangutan Is Born

Orangutan mothers give birth at night to a single baby, after an eight or nine-month pregnancy. Occasionally, a female orangutan may have twins. The mother is alone in her nest during the birth, but there may be an older son or daughter sleeping nearby. Once the baby is born, the mother cleans the infant. She then raises it to her breast so that it can suckle for the first time.

▲ A newborn orangutan is totally dependent on its mother. It cannot even raise its head. Within two weeks, it will have learned how to sit upright and use its hands.

The orangutan mother carries her baby, clutching it to her chest as she moves through the forest. Even though she has such a small baby, the mother continues to spend most of her time in the treetops, with the baby clinging on up to 100 ft. (30 m) above the ground.

▼ A mother orangutan is very protective of her baby. For the first two years of its life, a baby orangutan has constant physical contact with its mother.

BABY ORANGUTANS

A baby orangutan weighs about 3.3 lbs (1.5 kg) when it is born. Its eyes are open at birth, and it quickly learns to use its fingers to grip. However, it is still totally dependent on its mother.

●

The baby has big eyes, a very large head, and a very thin coat of hair. Its arms and legs are thin. These muscles do not start to develop until the orangutan begins climbing trees.

The bond between a female orangutan and her baby is the strongest of all relationships in orangutan society. The females are very good mothers and will do anything to care for and protect their young.

The mother carries her baby for the first year of its life. As the baby gets stronger, it will start to hold on by itself, either on its mother's chest or on her back. One of the reasons a mother carries her baby for so long is that it might fall if it tries to climb by itself.

▲ A mother clutches her young baby to her chest as she rests on a branch. When the baby is older, it will start to ride on its mother's back.

The mother keeps an eye out for predators. Adults have few natural enemies, but tigers occasionally attack them. Pigs have also been known to kill orangutan babies. Orangutans are in danger only when they are on the ground. This is another reason they spend so much time in the trees.

▼ The Sumatran tiger is Indonesia's largest predator. It will attack orangutans, but they often manage to escape by climbing into the trees.

Growing Up

◀ This baby is still living on its mother's milk. It will soon start tasting her food and learning which fruits are good to eat.

When it is about three months old, the baby orangutan begins eating soft fruit, as well as drinking its mother's milk. Sometimes the baby drinks water from its mother's mouth, or tastes some of her food.

The baby will not begin to move about by itself until it is at least one year old. Even then it will still be carried by its mother for much of the time and will continue to sleep in her nest.

Occasionally, two females will meet and spend some time together feeding. If both the females have babies, the babies will play together while their mothers eat.

▼ Perched on its mother's shoulders, a young orangutan is carried across a river. Orangutans cannot swim, so they usually avoid wading through water. Instead they swing across rivers using nearby trees.

As a juvenile, the young orangutan will no longer share its mother's night nest and must build its own. This young orangutan has built its night nest in a bamboo thicket.

Learning About Life

The mother begins to wean the young orangutan when it is three to four years old. At this age it is called a juvenile. Weaning can be a stressful time, with the juvenile screaming and throwing tantrums.

BUILDING A NIGHT NEST

Night nests are made by bending twigs over and weaving them together. The orangutan begins by making a circular platform. It then lines the platform with leaves and twigs. It can take up to 30 minutes to build a night nest from start to finish.

●

Young orangutans practice building nests from an early age. By the time they leave their mother's nest, they can make their own perfectly.

The orangutan youngster starts to build its own night nests at about this age. It will always be close to its mother's nest, perhaps even in the same tree. As it travels around with its mother, the young orangutan learns which foods are found where and at what time of year. It also learns how high it is safe to climb, how to move quickly through the trees, and all about the different forest sounds.

Sometimes the mother and juvenile encounter an adult male, who inspects the mother to see if she is ready to mate. The juvenile may be scared because the males are so large. Occasionally, the mother and juvenile will be accompanied by an older, adolescent orangutan that has left its own mother. These meetings teach the juvenile how to behave toward other orangutans.

▼ This orangutan can now climb by itself and use its hands and feet to hold food.

A Growing Family

The orangutan mother becomes pregnant again after mating with an adult male. She must make sure that the juvenile is completely weaned from her milk before she gives birth again. Pregnancy is a very dangerous time for her, because if food is not plentiful, she may become very weak.

The arrival of a brother or sister forces the juvenile into second place. The new baby is the mother's first concern, so the juvenile must start to look after itself. But it might still travel with its mother and her new baby.

▶ Orangutans use their feet like an extra pair of hands, holding onto trees and vines as they move through the forest.

▼ Orangutans get a lot of the water they need from the fruits that they eat. They also drink from rivers and streams. Young orangutans enjoy playing with water.

Finding Food

Orangutans depend on rain to find enough food. Tropical rain is very heavy. It comes in long storms called monsoons, which flood the swamp forests and make traveling on the ground almost impossible. The forest trees need the rain to produce flowers and fruit.

Different forest trees produce fruit at different times of the year. If there is not enough rain at the right time, some fruits may be scarce. The orangutans may have to go hungry for many months until another fruit comes into season.

▼ When it rains, orangutans cover their heads with large leaves or seek shelter. The huge roots at the base of a tree give some shelter to this damp youngster, but orangutans do not usually rest on the forest floor.

Orangutans find food partly by remembering where they found it last, but also by smelling and exploring. The orangutans must balance the quality of the food against the amount of time it takes to find it. Bark and leaves are plentiful and available all year-round, but they are not very nutritious. They are also difficult for the orangutans to digest. Seasonal fruits and flower nectar, which contain sugar, are sometimes harder to find. But they supply more energy and can be more easily absorbed by the body.

▲ The young orangutan learns which foods are good to eat by watching its mother.

An Orangutan's Diet

Although orangutans eat more than 400 different plants, or parts of plants, 90 percent of their diet consists of fruit. They are especially fond of a fruit called durian. To a human nose, durians smell horrible, but orangutans love them.

▼ Orangutans eat a variety of foods, from energy-rich fruits, seeds, and nectar to less-nutritious bark and leaves. They will also feed on insects, and will occasionally catch and eat small mammals, such as mice and lorises.

ORANGUTAN FOOD CHAIN

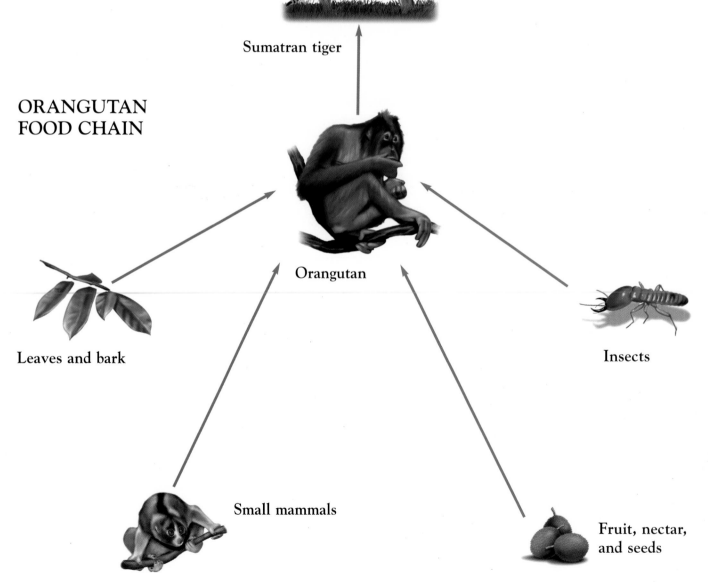

Sumatran tiger

Orangutan

Leaves and bark

Insects

Small mammals

Fruit, nectar, and seeds

Orangutans also eat flower nectar, honey, bark, leaves, termites, and fungi. They balance their diets just like people, making sure they get a mixture of sugars and fats (from fruit), carbohydrates (from leaves), and protein (from nuts). They sometimes eat mice and other small mammals, but meat does not seem to be a very important part of their diet.

▼ This orangutan has broken a piece off a termites' nest and is trying to fish out the insects with its tongue.

Leaving Home

By the time it is five or six years old, the orangutan has become an adolescent. It begins to spend more and more time away from its mother and her new child. Sometimes the adolescent moves around the forest alone, but at other times it travels with other females and their babies. It is becoming increasingly independent.

▼ This adolescent male is yawning, showing the developing canine teeth at the corners of his jaws. Orangutans use these teeth for cracking nuts open. The males also use them for fighting.

► The young orangutan will stay with its mother until it is six or seven years old. Then it will start to explore the forest on its own, before becoming fully independent.

A young male orangutan may want to mate with these females, but his advances will always be rejected. It will be another three or four years before he is accepted as an adult.

Female orangutans are lighter than males. They can flee from an adolescent male by moving into the higher, smaller branches of a tree. These branches will not hold the heavier adolescent.

The adolescent continues to learn social behavior from these encounters. It discovers for itself the signs that other orangutans make to show what mood they are in.

▲ Proboscis monkeys are known for their long noses. Like orangutans, they eat mainly fruit, but orangutans are larger than proboscis monkeys and will push them away from the best fruit trees.

Sharing the Forest

During its wanderings, the adolescent will also encounter other animals that live in the rain forest. Indonesia's rain forests are home to eagles, swifts, hornbills, and many other birds. There are also reptiles, such as snakes and crocodiles, and many mammals, including leopards, bats, porcupines, and proboscis monkeys. Thousands of insect species live there as well.

When it is about seven years old, the orangutan leaves its mother and becomes independent. Now it is called a subadult. A female subadult may share part of the area where her mother lives, called her home range. But a young male will move farther away from his birthplace.

Fully adult males will not tolerate a young male nearby. So the subadult must set off to find a home range of his own, which he can defend against male rivals.

▶ As males start to become subadults, they begin to develop cheek pads. Sumatran males, such as this one, may also grow shaggy beards.

Daily Life

All orangutans travel through the trees, moving from branch to branch and from trunk to trunk. They can walk along the thickest branches. To move from one branch to another, or between trees, orangutans use their feet like hands. They hold the first branch as they reach out to test the strength of the next branch. If the gap between the branches is too great, they will rock one branch so that it swings closer to the next one.

▶ The long arms of an orangutan help it to reach from one tree to another. But adult males like this one will not climb too high on such small trees.

Occasionally, orangutans miss a handhold and fall. But because they are very strong and graceful, they can usually break their fall by grabbing onto other, stronger branches. On rare occasions they may tumble all the way to the ground. A fall may injure or even kill a young orangutan, but adults are usually only bruised.

▶ Unlike females, adult males may travel on the ground, since some trees are not strong enough to take their weight. They usually walk on clenched fists, but they can walk upright if they need to.

An Orangutan's Day

The way orangutans spend their day depends on how much food is available. In total, they may spend up to six hours feeding or looking for food. If fruit is plentiful, they will take the opportunity to stuff themselves.

▲ The orangutan's teeth and jaws are very powerful. The orangutan strips leaves off branches by dragging them through its mouth.

Orangutans wake at dawn and leave their night nests to begin looking for food. Most days, they travel only half a mile (0.8 km) or less from their nest. They move from one food source to another depending upon which fruits are in season. Orangutans will visit the same tree again and again, until all its fruit is gone.

After a morning's feeding, orangutans build day nests, which are smaller than night nests. They rest in their day nests while they digest their food. Then in the afternoon, they feed again, either returning to the same tree or moving to a new one.

▼ A subadult orangutan resting in its day nest

Adulthood

Orangutan females reach adulthood earlier than males. Females become fully mature and capable of breeding at around seven years of age. But they rarely have their first baby until they are nine or ten.

Male orangutans are not fully mature until they are at least ten years old. When a male has established his own territory and is able to breed with females, he develops cheek pads.

▼ A male's cheek pads let females know that he is old enough to breed. They also probably help to scare away rival males. The cheek pads help the male orangutan make his loud, booming calls.

The area where an orangutan lives is known as its home range. A male's range is usually large, possibly from 2 to 3 sq. mi. (5 to 8 sq. km). There may be several females within a male's range, and the females' ranges may overlap. A female's home range only has to enclose enough food for her and her young. A male's range must enclose food for females with whom he can mate, and food for himself.

Young adult males that do not stay in one area but travel widely throughout the forest are called wanderers. Scientists are not sure whether these males eventually settle down when they find an unoccupied area, or whether they spend all their adult lives as wanderers.

▼ Male orangutans will fight to keep other males away from the females in their home ranges. You can see the fully developed canine teeth in this Sumatran male.

◀ This huge Bornean male is in the prime of his life. He is at least 25 years old and probably weighs over 198 lbs. (90 kg).

ORANGUTAN NOISES

Dominant males make a booming "long call" by inflating their throat pouches. It lasts for up to three minutes and can be heard more than half a mile (0.8 km) away. Males use this call to mark their territory and to attract females.

●

The fast call is similar to the long call, but is faster and sounds more urgent.

●

Annoyed orangutans purse their lips and make a smacking noise called a kiss-squeak.

Courtship and Breeding

Mating can take place at any time of year. It depends on whether the female is ready to become pregnant and whether she likes the dominant male. This is the time when male orangutans are most likely to fight, as each tries to gain access to the female.

If a male meets a willing female and she accepts him, he will court her. During courtship the pair move around the forest together, sharing food, remaining close to one another, and often touching. The courtship period may be very short, sometimes lasting little more than a day.

Mating may occur many times during the courtship and can occur on the ground, in the trees, or even hanging from a branch. Once courtship and mating are over, the male leaves the female. He takes no further part in the birth or rearing of his baby.

Female orangutans continue to breed throughout their adult lives, but they usually only have three or four young. This slow breeding rate makes it difficult for orangutans to increase their numbers.

► A female orangutan in Sumatra

Old Age

Orangutans have long lives, sometimes reaching over 50 years of age. Some orangutans die early from illness and disease. Others may die from starvation if food is particularly scarce. They have no natural predators except for tigers and leopards, which sometimes kill infants and adult females.

Old orangutans prefer to avoid meeting others and are rarely seen in the wild. Old males are probably too weak to fight, so they may give up their territory to younger orangutans.

▶ An old female orangutan. Like the males, female orangutans gradually become slower and weaker as they get older.

▼ An adult male's cheek pads may be scarred and torn as a result of fighting with other males.

Threats

Unfortunately, the orangutan is not safe in its forest world. Its numbers have fallen by about 80 percent since 1900. No one is quite sure how many orangutans are left in the wild, but estimates range from 15,000 to 20,000.

The main threat to Indonesia's orangutans is the destruction of their rain forest habitat. The forest trees are being cut down for timber, and the land is being cleared for mining. As new settlements spring up, more forest is turned into farmland.

▼ The wood from tropical trees is very valuable. This encourages people to cut the trees down for timber. People then use the land for farming, which makes it impossible for the forest to recover.

In 1997, raging fires swept through the orangutans' forests. The fires were deliberately started by people who wanted the land for farming. The fires got out of control and spread rapidly. They burned for more than a month and destroyed more than 385 sq. mi. (1,000 sq. km) of forest.

▲ While the tallest and strongest trees may survive a fire, most of the forest is destroyed. Many of the animals that live in it are killed as well.

The Indonesian government is aware of the problems the orangutans face. It has made some forest areas into national parks and wildlife preserves. The orangutans can live in these areas undisturbed by human activity.

The Pet Trade

In some countries, people like to keep baby orangutans as pets. To capture a baby, hunters must first shoot its mother. This is very disturbing to the infant, and it is quite likely to die of shock.

Even if the young orphan survives capture, it may die on its way to its new owner. It is illegal to take orangutans out of Indonesia, so they must be smuggled out. They are often taken in small crates or packages with false labels.

▼ Many people think young apes are cute. This young chimpanzee and orangutan are being raised together as pets. But the pet trade threatens both species.

The few orangutans that survive the journey face a difficult life. People only like to keep them as pets when they are small, but once an orangutan has grown larger and stronger, it may be abandoned or sold to a zoo. All conservation organizations agree that orangutans are not suitable to keep as pets. There is an international effort to stop this trade.

▲ Because they are intelligent, orangutans can be taught to perform many tricks. Like the pet trade, collecting animals for circuses threatens wild populations.

Orangutan Conservation

Some orangutans live in zoos that look after them well and try to make their lives as natural as possible. This is difficult, because few zoos have access to all the wild fruits that an orangutan would normally eat. Also, wild orangutans usually live alone, but in zoos they are forced to live with other orangutans.

▼ Many orangutans are kept in zoos around the world. Now that orangutans have bred successfully in captivity, it is no longer necessary for zoos to collect more animals from the wild.

Despite this, many orangutans have gotten used to living with each other in zoos and have managed to breed successfully. Breeding in zoos is called captive breeding. Some people believe captive breeding plays an important part in conservation. It helps to maintain orangutan numbers at a time when some wild populations are threatened with extinction. However, others think it is better to return orangutans to the wild than to breed them in captivity.

Zoos also play an important role in educating the public. What better way to learn about orangutans than seeing how they behave in person?

▲ This orangutan orphan will have to live in captivity until he is old enough to be released back into the wild. While he is in captivity, he needs to be fed as natural a diet as possible.

Rehabilitation

Some orangutans have been returned to the wild in a process called rehabilitation. Many of these orangutans were once pets. Others were taken from smugglers, and some were orphaned when their mothers were killed in forest fires.

In the wild, the orphans' mothers would have taught them the skills they needed, such as how to make a night nest and what fruits to eat. Without their mothers, the baby orangutans must learn from people. Rehabilitation centers are usually located in national parks, where the orangutans will be safe from hunters when they are released.

▲ These orangutans are at a rehabilitation center. They are not used to finding their own fruit in the trees, so the wardens at the center give them extra food. Once the orangutans have learned to fend for themselves in the wild, they will no longer need this extra food.

DISEASE

Orangutans can catch many human diseases. Orangutans' bodies are not used to our diseases, so they get sicker than we do.

●

Rehabilitation centers must be sure that sickness does not spread between orphans and, most important, from orphans to the wild population. Quarantine is the word for the process of keeping sick animals away from healthy ones.

Most rehabilitated orangutans become only semiwild, and occasionally return to the rehabilitation center to feed. However, a few do become truly wild and spend the rest of their lives in the forest. Many tourists come to the rehabilitation centers to see orangutans. This helps to pay for the orphans' food and the wages of the national park wardens, who protect the wild orangutans and their forest home.

You will find a list of wildlife groups trying to help orangutans on page 47.

▼ Orangutans must be healthy before they are returned to the forest. The youngsters are weighed regularly to check that they are growing at a normal pace.

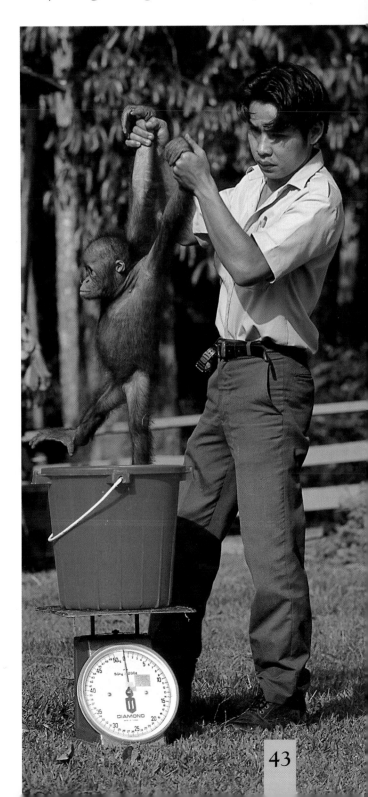

Orangutan Life Cycle

 A single baby orangutan is born after an eight- or nine-month pregnancy. The mother is alone when she gives birth. The baby suckles its mother's milk.

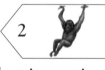 The baby begins to eat solid food after three or four months, but it continues to suckle for another three years. For the first year of its life, it is carried everywhere by its mother.

 When the orangutan is four years old and a juvenile, its mother weans it off her milk. Females may give birth every four or five years.

At age five or six, the adolescent orangutan begins to spend more time away from its mother and her second baby. Occasionally, it may travel with another female and her baby.

4

By seven years of age, the orangutan is a subadult and independent. A subadult female may live near its mother, but a male subadult moves farther away.

5

Female orangutans have their first baby at about ten years old. Males are not fully adult until they are almost fourteen. Then they develop huge cheek pads and compete to become the dominant male in a territory. Orangutans can live for more than fifty years.

6

Glossary

Adolescence The age of animals just before they become adults.

Canine teeth Large, sharp teeth used for biting and fighting.

Carbohydrates Substances found in food. Carbohydrates give the body energy.

Courtship Animal behavior that leads to mating.

Diterocarp A class of tropical trees in Asia.

Dominant Commanding a territory.

Habitat The place where an animal or plant naturally lives.

Home range An area of land used by an animal but not defended as a territory.

Juvenile An orangutan between three and five years old.

Mammal An animal that feeds its young on milk.

Nectar A sugary liquid made by flowers.

Opposable thumbs Thumbs positioned opposite the fingers, so the hand can grip.

Orphan A young animal whose parents have died.

Predator An animal that kills and eats other animals.

Proteins Substances, found in food, that the body needs to grow and build muscles.

Quarantine A system in which sick animals are kept apart from healthy ones.

Rehabilitation The process of returning a captive animal to the wild.

Smuggling Moving animals between countries illegally.

Species A group of animals or plants with similar features that can breed together.

Suckling Drinking a mother's milk.

Territory An area that an animal defends.

Wean A mother weans her baby when she stops letting it drink her milk.

Further Information

Organizations to Contact

International Primate Protection League (IPPL)
P.O. Box 766
Summerville, SC 29484
(843) 871-2280
www.ippl.org

Orangutan Foundation International
822 S. Wellesley Avenue
Los Angeles, CA 90049
(310) 207-1655
www.orangutan.org

The Primate Conservation & Welfare Society
P.O. Box 2101
Port Townsend, WA 98368
www.primates-online.com

World Wildlife Fund
1250 Twenty-Fourth Street, N.W.
P.O. Box 97180
Washington, DC 20077-7180
www.worldwildlife.org

Books to Read

Gallardo, Evelyn. *Among the Orangutans: The Birute Galdikas Story*. Chronicle, 1993.

Horton, Casey. *Apes* (Endangered). Benchmark, 1996.

Miller-Schroeder, Pat. *Gorillas* (Untamed World). Raintree Steck-Vaughn, 1997.

Redmond, Ian. *Gorilla, Monkey & Ape* (Eyewitness Books). Knopf, 1995.

Robinson, Claire. *Chimpanzees* (In the Wild). Heinemann, 1996.

Russon, Anne E. *Orangutans: Wizards of the Rain Forest*. Firefly, 2000.

Index

All the numbers in **bold** refer to photographs or illustrations.

DATE DUE
